From Rubbish to Riches

Buttons and Beads

Daniel Nunn

www.raintreepublishers.co.uk
Visit our website to find out more information about Raintree books.

To order:
☎ Phone 0845 6044371
🖹 Fax +44 (0) 1865 312263
🖳 Email myorders@raintreepublishers.co.uk

Customers from outside the UK please telephone +44 1865 312262

Raintree is an imprint of Capstone Global Library Limited, a company incorporated in England and Wales having its registered office at 7 Pilgrim Street, London, EC4V 6LB – Registered company number: 6695582

Edited by Rebecca Rissman, Daniel Nunn, and Sian Smith
Designed by Joanna Hinton-Malivoire
Picture research by Tracy Cummins
Originated by Capstone Global Library Ltd
Printed and bound in China by South China Printing Company Ltd

ISBN 978 1 406 22680 5 (hardback)
15 14 13 12 11
10 9 8 7 6 5 4 3 2 1

ISBN 978 1 406 22687 4 (paperback)
16 15 14 13 12
10 9 8 7 6 5 4 3 2 1

British Library Cataloguing in Publication Data
Nunn, Daniel. Buttons and beads.
(From rubbish to riches)
1. Button craft–Juvenile literature. 2. Beadwork
3. Trash art 4. Refuse and refuse disposal 5. Salvage
745.5'8-dc22
A full catalogue record for this book is available from the British Library.

Acknowledgements
We would like to thank the following for permission to reproduce photographs: Heinemann Raintree pp. 4, 5, 6, 8, 9, 10, 11, 12, 13, 14, 15, 16, 17, 18, 19, 20, 21, 22, 23a, 23b (Karon Dubke); istockphoto pp. 7 (© Rob Hill), 23e (© Mostafa Hefni); Shutterstock pp. 23c (© Jaren Jai Wicklund), 23d (© Denis and Yulia Pogostins).

Cover photograph of flowers in homemade vases reproduced with permission of Photolibrary (Radius Images). Cover inset image of buttons and beads and back cover images of a bracelet and flowers reproduced with permission of Heinemann Raintree (Karon Dubke).

Every effort has been made to contact copyright holders of material reproduced in this book. Any omissions will be rectified in subsequent printings if notice is given to the publisher.

Contents

Some words are shown in bold, **like this**. You can
find them in the glossary on page 23.

What are buttons and beads?

A bead is a small round object with a hole through the middle.

Beads are used to make necklaces or to **decorate** clothes.

A button is a small object used to **fasten** clothes.

Buttons and beads can be made from lots of different **materials**.

What happens when you throw buttons and beads away?

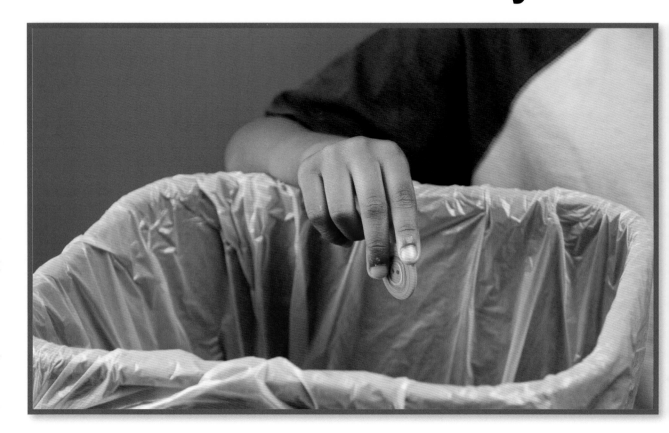

Buttons and beads can look nice and be very useful.

But when you have finished with them, do you throw them away?

If so, then your buttons and beads will end up at a rubbish tip.

They will be buried in the ground and may stay there for a very long time.

How can I reuse old buttons and beads?

You can use old buttons and beads to make your own new things.

When you have finished with a button or a bead, put it somewhere safe.

Soon you will have lots of buttons and beads waiting to be reused.

You are ready to turn your rubbish into riches!

What can I make with buttons and beads?

Buttons and beads can be turned into beautiful jewellery.

These beads have been made into a bracelet.

You can also use buttons and beads to make rings, necklaces, and other jewellery.

They can be whatever colour you want!

This picture has been put together using old buttons.

Can you make your own button or bead art?

These flowers have been made with buttons, too!

They would make a perfect Mother's Day present.

What can I decorate with buttons and beads?

Buttons and beads make brilliant decorations.

You can use them to make clothes look nicer.

You can also use them to **decorate** boxes.

Why not turn a boring old box into something you want to keep?

You can use buttons to **decorate** old flowerpots.

Try to find buttons that will match the colour of the flowers you made earlier.

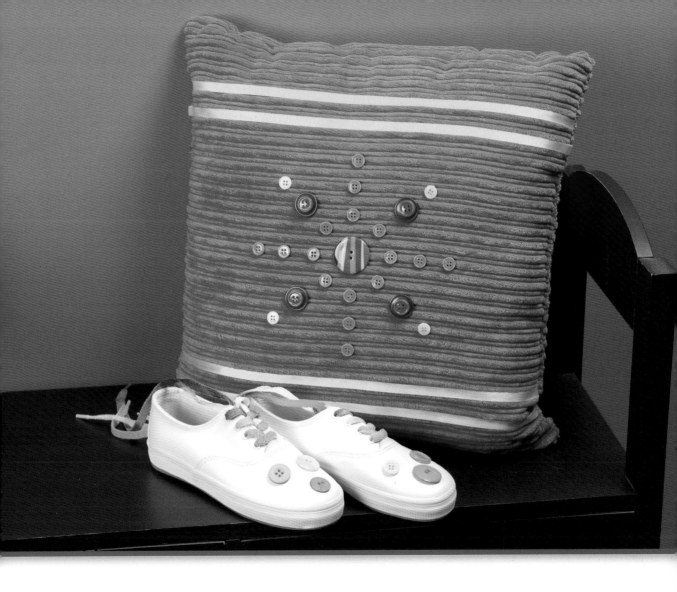

In fact, you can use buttons and beads
to decorate almost anything!

Make your own button and bead creatures

You can use buttons and beads to make some very strange creatures.

You will need buttons, beads, **pipe cleaners**, googly eyes, and craft glue.

First, use your **imagination** to decide what sort of creature you would like to make.

Then start to thread the pipe cleaners through the buttons and beads.

Next, twist the **pipe cleaners** into different shapes to make your creature's body parts.

You could make arms, legs, wings, tails, horns, or shells.

Finally, use the craft glue to stick some eyes on your creature.

Now it's time to make your creature some friends. You could make a whole zoo!

Button game

If you've got any buttons left, you could play a game of tiddlywinks!

To play, fire small buttons into a cup by pressing them with a large button.

Glossary

 **decorate** add something fancy to something plain to make it look nicer

 **fasten** do something up or tie something together

 **imagination** thinking up ideas or seeing pictures of things in your head

 **material** what something is made of

 **pipe cleaner** piece of bendy wire covered in fluffy material

Find out more

Ask an adult to help you make fun things with buttons and beads using the websites below.

Button pictures: **www.bhg.com/crafts/kids/rainy-day/ kids-crafts-buttons/?page=4**

Flowers: **pbskids.org/zoom/activities/do/ buttonflowers.html**

Jewellery: **familyfun.go.com/crafts/bedazzling- beaded-jewelry-845038/**

You can find other ideas at: **crafts.kaboose.com/ wear/bead-crafts.html**

Index